Find your ideal job using LinkedIn

An easy step-by-step guide

2020 Edition

Contents:

Introduction

Whether you're new to LinkedIn or you are already an active member, if you are thinking about switching jobs, this book will help you get the most out of the world's largest professional network and make its superior technology work for you.
The aim of this book is to be straight to the point and to simplify every step, so you can get started right away.

I recommend you read the first two chapters to fully understand why LinkedIn is such a big asset in your job search, and how you can make its advanced technology work for you.

If you are a LinkedIn novice, chapter 3 will guide you through setting up a profile and a short overview of LinkedIn's basic functions; you may want to only skim or even skip this chapter if you already have an established profile.

In chapter 4, you will learn how to optimise your profile for LinkedIn's technology, in order to receive the most suitable job suggestions for you, and to make sure you can be found by recruiters.

Chapters 5 and 6 will teach you how to signal your availability without your boss knowing you are on the job hunt, how to specify your expectations, and how to work with job suggestions, how to search for jobs and set search alerts.

Finally, chapter 7 will address common questions not covered in the chapters above, as well as basic netiquette.

So without further ado, let's get started on finding your ideal job with LinkedIn!

Chapter 1:
Why use LinkedIn for your job search

LinkedIn is the biggest professional network worldwide. As of February 2020, it has over 675 million members in over 200 countries and territories worldwide, with over 183 million located in the US and Canada, over 206 million in Europe, and over 11 million in Australia. This, coupled with LinkedIn being the top platform where people enter their professional data, makes it a great place for employers (and recruitment agencies) to find the talent they are looking for.

For actual jobseekers, LinkedIn's unique data matching and AI technology offers another advantage that other platforms currently cannot yet compete with: it will serve up the most suitable roles for you automatically. This means you can easily identify jobs you are a great fit for, and therefore have a higher chance to be called for an interview.

There are two ways of how you can find your next opportunity with LinkedIn: applying directly for jobs, and signalling your availability to recruiters that actively search the network for potential employees.

In order to make the technology work for you for either method, it is imperative that you have a strong

LinkedIn profile set up, which we will cover in Chapter 4.

Chapter 2:
Understanding LinkedIn's technology

LinkedIn's technology is so unique because of the wealth of data the network provides. Most LinkedIn members are not on the platform to find employment, but rather to excel at their current job (through industry news and insights, making meaningful new connections or researching companies), to stay in touch with business connections and fellow students, or to future proof their skillsets by using LinkedIn's learning platform.

LinkedIn's technology draws data from members' profiles (location, job title, industry, skillsets, keywords etc), from their members' expressed preferences (e.g. following certain companies or industry topics), but also from their members' actions on the platform (e.g. checking out certain company pages or interacting with their employees). LinkedIn can also aggregate this data to discover trends, such as skills surplus areas or skill shortages, or how certain professional groups move globally.

It's important to understand that no one can view or track your personal activity- the technology itself matches your data to serve you with the most relevant articles, updates and job opportunities.

Just as LinkedIn works for you to show the most relevant opportunities, this also allows companies to find and contact the candidates that are the closest fit to their specific requirements.

Therefore having a solid profile presence is paramount- otherwise the matching technology cannot work for you.

Chapter 3:
Setting up an account, and first steps on LinkedIn

If you have an existing LinkedIn profile, you may wish to skip this section.

Before you set up your account, you should have the following ready: your resume, a good headshot photo, and access to your email to confirm during the sign up process.

Setting up your account is easy:
- Log on to www.linkedin.com
- Go to sign up and follow the steps (this will include confirming your email address)

Ensure you enter your real name, location etc. You are creating your professional online identity, so nicknames will not do you any favours.

If you are worried about your current employers discovering your profile, don't be. As mentioned, LinkedIn is not a job-hunting channel, but an online network of professionals. Unless you explicitly state it on your profile, your employers will not be able to see whether you are on the lookout for new opportunities (more detail on this in chapter 5).

NB: During sign up, and on later occasions, LinkedIn will repeatedly ask whether you want to invite people from your email address book. While this may seem tempting, I recommend you decline unless you intend to send automated invitations to your mother-in-law, your vet, and anyone else you may have saved in your emails.

Building your profile step by step:

We will optimise your profile in Chapter 4.
For now, you want to build a good-looking, informative profile, so let's go through each of the sections.

Profile Photo:

This should go without saying, but choose a well-lit, professional but approachable photo. No group pictures (or pictures showing parts of cropped out people), and no beer in hand. LinkedIn recommend a headshot with a friendly smile- remember that this is the first impression people will get of you. Unless your work environment requires it, there is no need to dress overly formal. Think about how you want your existing (and future!) colleagues to see you as a person.

Tagline:

Often a mystery to LinkedIn newbies, the tagline frequently gets neglected or simply filled with their current job title. The tagline is a short way to introduce yourself to the world and tell people what you do in very few words.
Imagine you're explaining your job to your grandma, and- where appropriate- add a small dose of humour-

anything from "I design iconic landmarks" (Civil Engineer) to "helping you achieve your best shape ever" (Personal Trainer) works well.

Summary:

a few short sentences about what you do, but most importantly: what drives you. When people read your profile, they love to understand your passions, why you do what you do, and where you are hoping to be.

The ideal summary can be skimmed in about 30 seconds, contains lots of relevant keywords to give an understanding of what you do, and gives a glimpse of your personality and motivations.

Here too, a little humour can go a long way to make you much more approachable. Here's a possible example for an Accountant:
"A real numbers geek by heart, I have worked for some of the biggest names in the Accounting world. I thrive on getting the job done and have loved spreadsheets from day one. In my spare time, I apply my skills in pro-bono work for charities, and am looking for my next big challenge, preferably in the nonprofit sector."
Be careful- you may want to skip that last part if you don't want your current boss to know that you're on the lookout.

You can add contact details in your summary, but be mindful to only do so if it gives you a real advantage (e.g. generating new business leads), as your contact details will be visible to complete strangers if you put them in this public section.

People and potential employers will still be able to message you via "InMail" (LinkedIn's messaging service) without getting access to your private contact details.

Experience:

This is where your resume will come in handy to fill in the timeline. Each job, or at least the last three/ most recent years should have a paragraph or bullet point section (your pick) about your tasks and achievements. We will finetune these in Chapter 4, so don't worry too much about the contents for now.

Hot tip: If applicable to your line of work, you can add media items such as a portfolio, published article, website, videos etc. to each experience section. Having this readily available can give you an extra advantage over other applicants.

You'll find the "add media" option in the "Edit experience" section.

Skills:

This section is very important if you are looking to be found or want LinkedIn's technology to serve up the most suitable jobs for you. Depending on your desired position, these may be soft skills (business management, customer support etc) or hard skills (Javascript, AutoCAD etc).

Ideally you should have a mix of both to represent your skillset. Pick from LinkedIn's suggested list if possible, as this is the same list of options recruiters will use to find a match. Over time, you may see your connections endorsing you for these skills; endorsements are a great signal to business partners/ peers/ potential employers that you do possess these skills.

Education, Licences and Certifications:

many positions require a specific education level or professional certificates, so ensure to list your educational details/ professional qualifications. This also includes qualifications such as Working with Children, forklift driving licence etc.

Volunteer experience:

Research shows that volunteering work makes you stand out as a candidate and can even count as much as actual work experience if you are still new to the working world.

Recommendations:

Recommendations are as good as references on your CV. Ask previous employers/ peers/ clients to leave you a recommendation, and do return the favour.

Voila! Your basic LinkedIn profile is complete. Next, you will need to add connections.
Start by searching for peers/ clients/ even friends in the search bar and clicking connect. You can even add a few words (especially if the person may not remember you too well).

You can also search for companies you like and start following them, as well as influential people in the business world. If you want to learn more about a specific company as an employer, see if they have activated the "Life" tab on their company page which offers valuable insights.

Once you have made connections/ follow companies and people, your newsfeed on the start page will start filling up. You may also start seeing ads for job opportunities on your home page. Are they a good match or do you need to add information?

Hold your horses applying for jobs until we have optimised your profile, to ensure you aren't wasting your energy on jobs that aren't entirely suitable for you.

LinkedIn quick start for beginners:

In this next section, I want to give you a short overview of how to use LinkedIn as a beginner to get benefit out of the network, outside of just finding a new job.

Homepage:

your homepage will display a newsfeed of mainly people/ topics you follow. Occasionally, you may also see relevant articles or marketing targeted to you, based on your profile data.

You can like, comment on or share what you see in your newsfeed.

At the very top of your Homepage, you can share your own thoughts, links to interesting articles etc.

If you want to be seen as an industry thought leader, you can even write a long-form article.

Whatever you do, ensure that you portray yourself from your best professional angle. Be courteous when you comment, and refrain from sharing riddles or funny cat pictures.

Potential employers (and business partners/ colleagues/ your current boss) can see what you post, so before you hit that button, think about whether the contents or thoughts you're about to share are of value to others.

Account settings:
You'll find this section in the "Me" section at the top menu bar (it shows a small profile picture). Here, you can determine exactly who can view your profile, your activity etc. Be mindful not to restrict access (or contacting ability) too much while you are looking for your net career move- you want to leave communication channels open for recruiters to contact you.

Help & Support:
Under the "Me" section, you will find an "Open Quick Help" link, where you can type a question or contact LinkedIn's online help team if necessary.
Be prepared for a few days' wait time, as LinkedIn's membership is growing exponentially, increasing the number of help requests logged daily. Most answers can be easily found by using the search function.

LinkedIn App:
The LinkedIn app is free and great to connect and get updates on the go. Especially for job hunters, it is a handy tool to have as you can get job alerts, research companies and apply at any time.

Chapter 4:
Optimising your LinkedIn profile for job matching

We've covered how LinkedIn's matching technology selects the most suitable jobs for you, and how it empowers recruiters to find and contact you for the roles they are looking to fill.

In this section, we'll explore how you can optimise your profile to get the best results from this technology.

LinkedIn matches job opportunities to you based on several factors, including job title, keywords, skillset, industry, location and more.
To start, I'd like you to make a list of the skills you possess, focussing on the skills you are likely to need in the role you would like to work in. From here, think about alternative names or spelling for those skills (e.g. Java or JavaScript).

When completing your LinkedIn profile, ensure to include these skillsets and alternative descriptions both in the flow text of your Experience section, as well as in the Skills section.
If you hold an unusual job title, consider changing it to a more generic version to increase your matches further and make it easier for recruiters to understand

what you do. "Chief of Happiness" may be a great title, but is unlikely to find many matches on roles posted (and yes, this is a real job title).

Example: Possible Keywords/ Skills

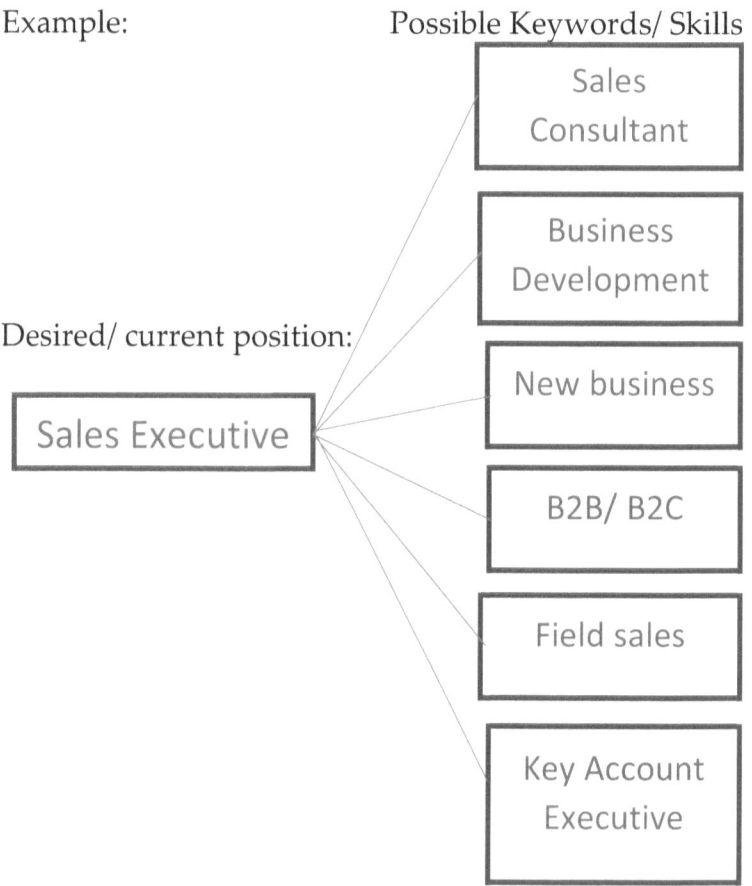

You will find empty notes pages at the end of this book to make your own list of keywords.

Chapter 5:
Signal your availability to Recruiters

Undoubtedly you are now keen to get started with your job search.

Before you do this, I encourage you to signal to recruiters that you are open to hearing from them. This increases your chances of being contacted by a recruiter via "InMail" dramatically.
InMail is LinkedIn's messaging system, and many recruiters use this function to shoulder tap suitable candidates.

To switch on this function, go to your own profile. In the top section, you will find a box saying "**Show recruiters you're open** to opportunities…".
Follow the "Get started" link, which enables you to select preferred job titles, locations and visibility.
If you are concerned about your boss seeing that you are on the job hunt, choose visibility "Recruiters only". This way, only recruiters at other companies (not your own employers) will be able to see that you are available for a new challenge.

To make sure all data is up to date, LinkedIn will ask you whether you are still looking after 90 days, if you changed jobs or if you haven't responded to messages from recruiters (it is always recommended to respond to a recruiters' message, even if you're not interested. You never know where your paths may cross again in the future.).

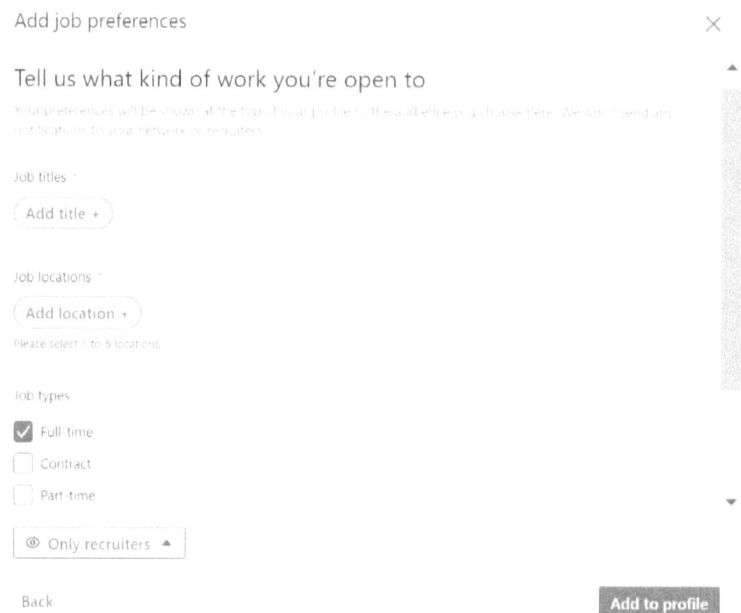

Chapter 6:
Searching jobs- job suggestions, job search, job alerts

Now that your profile has been optimised, you will start seeing relevant job suggestions being pushed into your home page newsfeed.

You will also notice display ads for job opportunities showing on your homepage, or across your LinkedIn experience- these are targeting you specifically based on your profile and actions, so they are worthwhile clicking on to learn more.

You can now click on "Jobs", where you will automatically see the most suitable jobs being suggested, based on your profile data, preferences and actions. If you are willing to pay for a premium account (you don't need to; see Chapter 7), you will even see jobs where you are in the top 10% of applicants.

If you are finding the jobs aren't a good match, bear in mind that artificial intelligence can only use what we feed it, and chances are you may need to optimise your profile again with the right keywords.

For example, if your job title only states: "Engineer", and your profile doesn't expand on what you do on a day-to-day basis, you may see civil engineering jobs being presented to an IT Engineer and vice versa.

In the top row of the Jobs section, you can also adjust your Career Interests, either by updating your preferences shown to recruiters (see Chapter 5), and even by entering an address to show you commute times for the jobs you view.

Finally, while you shouldn't need to, you can search for specific jobs using the search bar, just as you would on a standard job board.
This can be useful if you are looking to make a lateral career move or want to move to another location.
If you look up jobs via search, LinkedIn will in the future serve up similar jobs to support your goals.

Responding to suggested jobs instead of searching gives you a bigger competitive advantage, as you have been pre-matched to the role, and therefore your chances of securing an interview are much higher than via job search.

When you look at a job, you can either save it for later or apply with your profile (unless the company insists on directing you elsewhere, it should be as easy as hitting the apply button once and confirming).

You can also set search alerts for similar jobs (on the top right).

Chapter 7:
Commonly asked questions and netiquette tips

Q: Do I need to sign up for a premium/ job seeker account?

A: In short, no. A paid account upgrade does give you interesting insights, such as how high you rank as a match compared to other applicants and additional company insights. Generally speaking though, you can find all the relevant information you need via the job descriptions, the company page (and "Life" tab), and- provided you have switched on the function- recruiters will still be able to see that you are open to new opportunities, thus increasing your chances of receiving an InMail from a recruiter.

Q: Should I always reply to a recruiter, even if I am not interested in their offer?

A: Yes, please do. The person has taken the time to review your profile, determined they are interested in speaking with you, and reached out. It's only polite to respond, even if it is to say that this is not the role you are after. Also, you never know if you don't meet the same recruiter somewhere else further down the road!

Q: Can I change my setting so I can be contacted by company recruiters, but not by recruitment agencies?

A: Unfortunately, there is no setting for this right now. If you are actively job hunting, you may wish to speak with agencies also. The best way to discourage agency recruiters if you'd prefer to hear directly from companies only is to add a note in your preferences saying "no agency recruiters please".

Q: Should I put "available for work" in my profile tag line?

A: This is common practice and may send extra opportunities your way (for example, one of your connections might see it and refer you). I recommend still adding what you do and injecting a little personality, e.g.: "Java developer extraordinaire- now available for my next opportunity". Also do remember this is publicly visible to everyone, including your current boss.

Q: How do I increase my visibility and chances of getting noticed?

A: The more you network (like, comment on, share contents) or publish yourself (industry news, relevant articles etc), the more people will take note and check out your profile. This increases your chances of getting noticed by recruiters, or by people who can refer you for a role. Be mindful that LinkedIn is a professional network, so ensure you are always respectful, friendly and add value or insights. Keep any urges to leave negative comments to yourself as it may reflect negatively on you.

Conclusion:

The above is all you need to find your ideal job with LinkedIn. Make sure you check job suggestions regularly, or set up job alerts directly to your email.

Even after you have found your next role, LinkedIn is a useful asset to connect with colleagues, peers and business partners, to stay up to date with industry news, and perhaps you even want to try LinkedIn's learning section to upskill yourself for career progression.

Best of luck with your job search!

Notes:

_____

_____

_____

_____

_____

_____

_____

_____

_____

_____

_____

_____

Notes:

_____

_____

_____

_____

_____

_____

_____

_____

_____

_____

_____

_____

www.ingramcontent.com/pod-product-compliance
Lightning Source LLC
Chambersburg PA
CBHW030601220526

45463CB00007B/3137